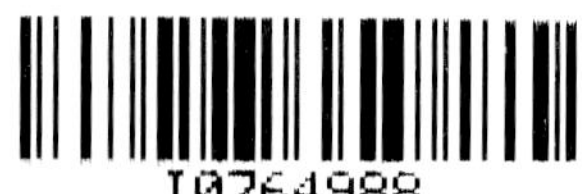

Relaxing Nature
An Adult Coloring Book

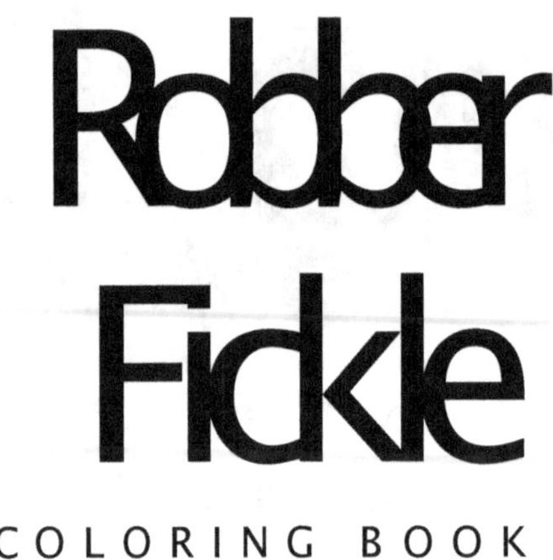

For Any Question and Suggestions
robberfickle@gmail.com

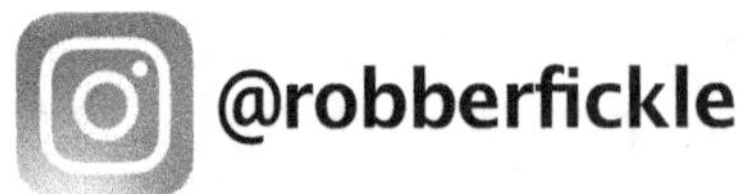

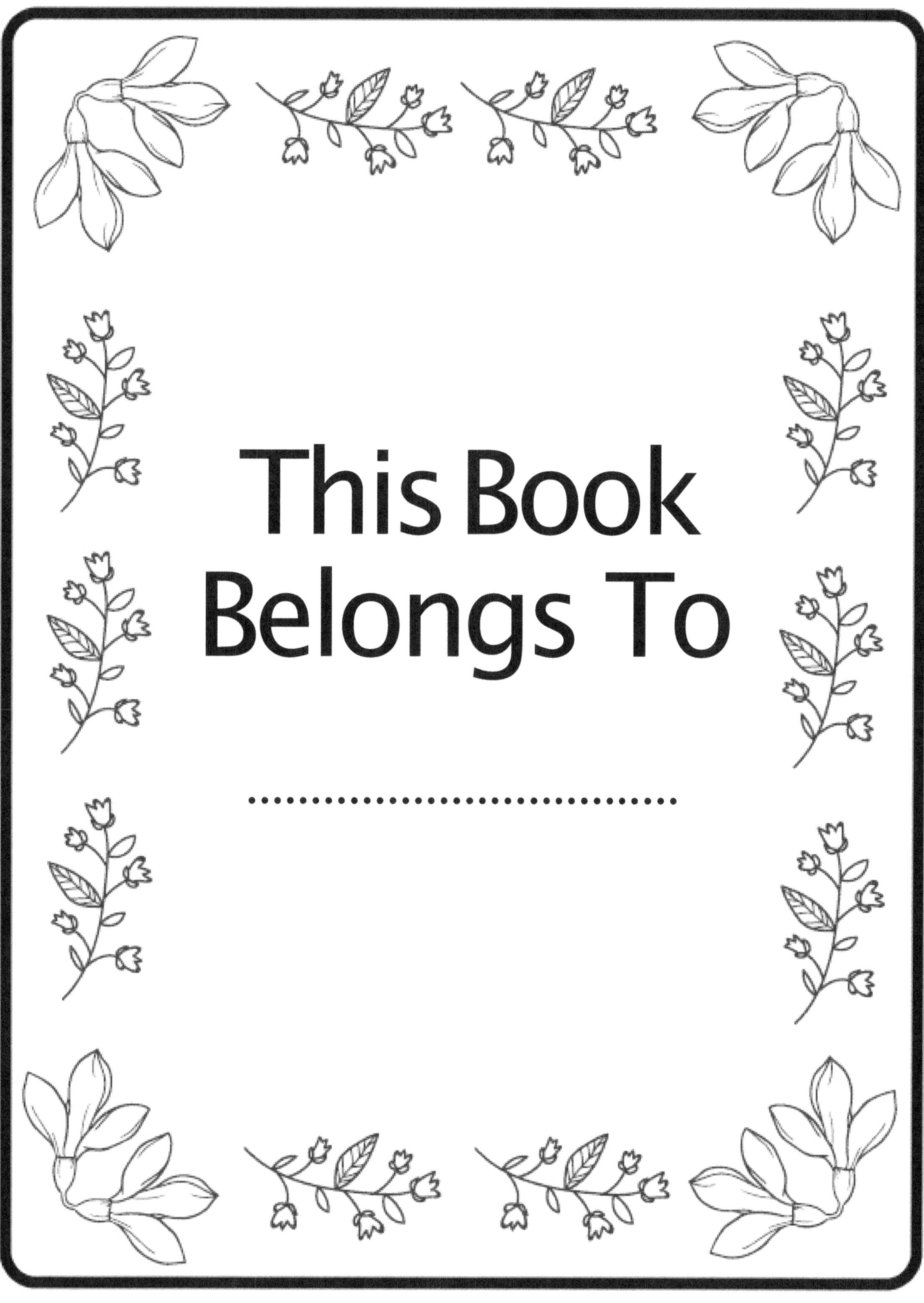

This Book Belongs To

....

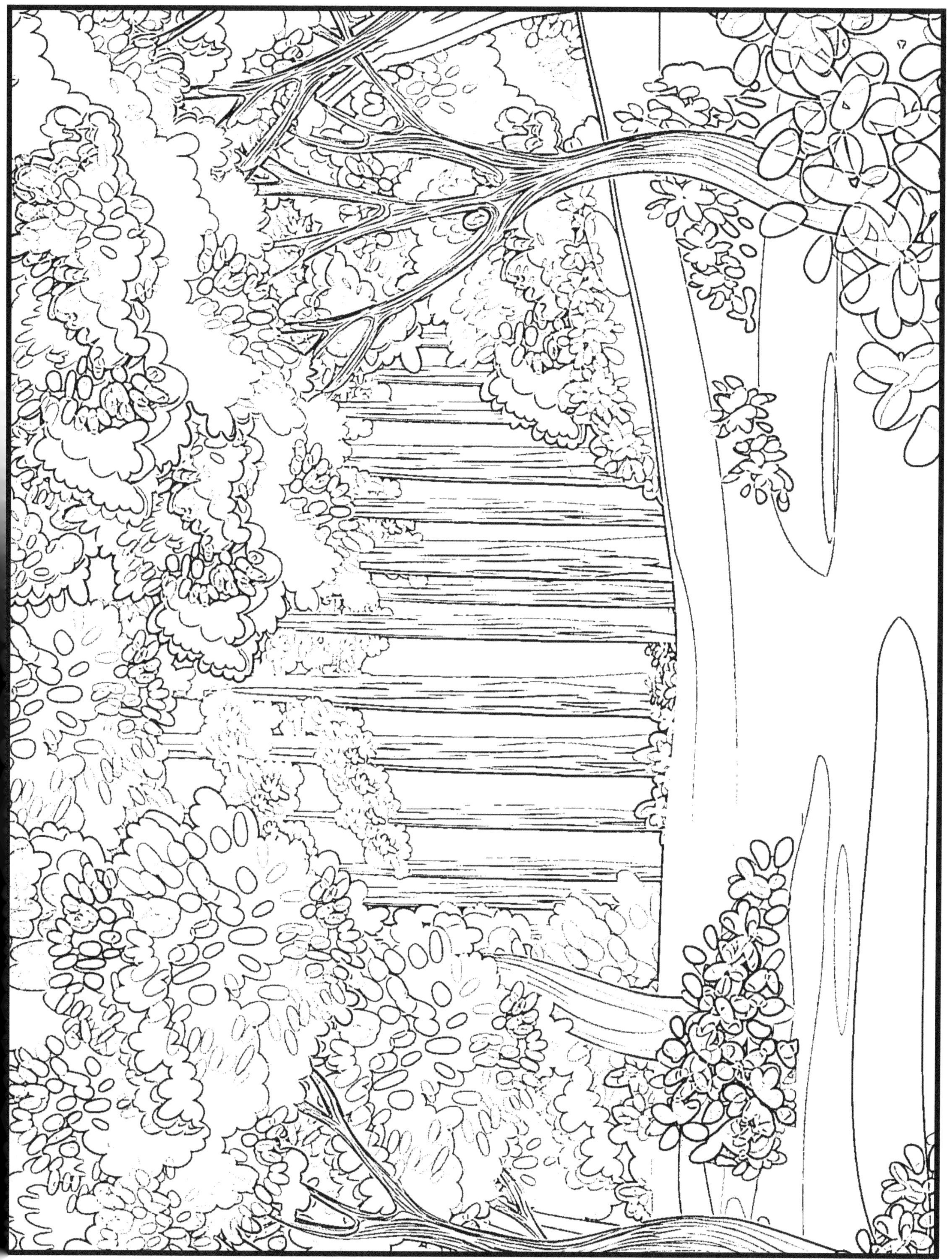

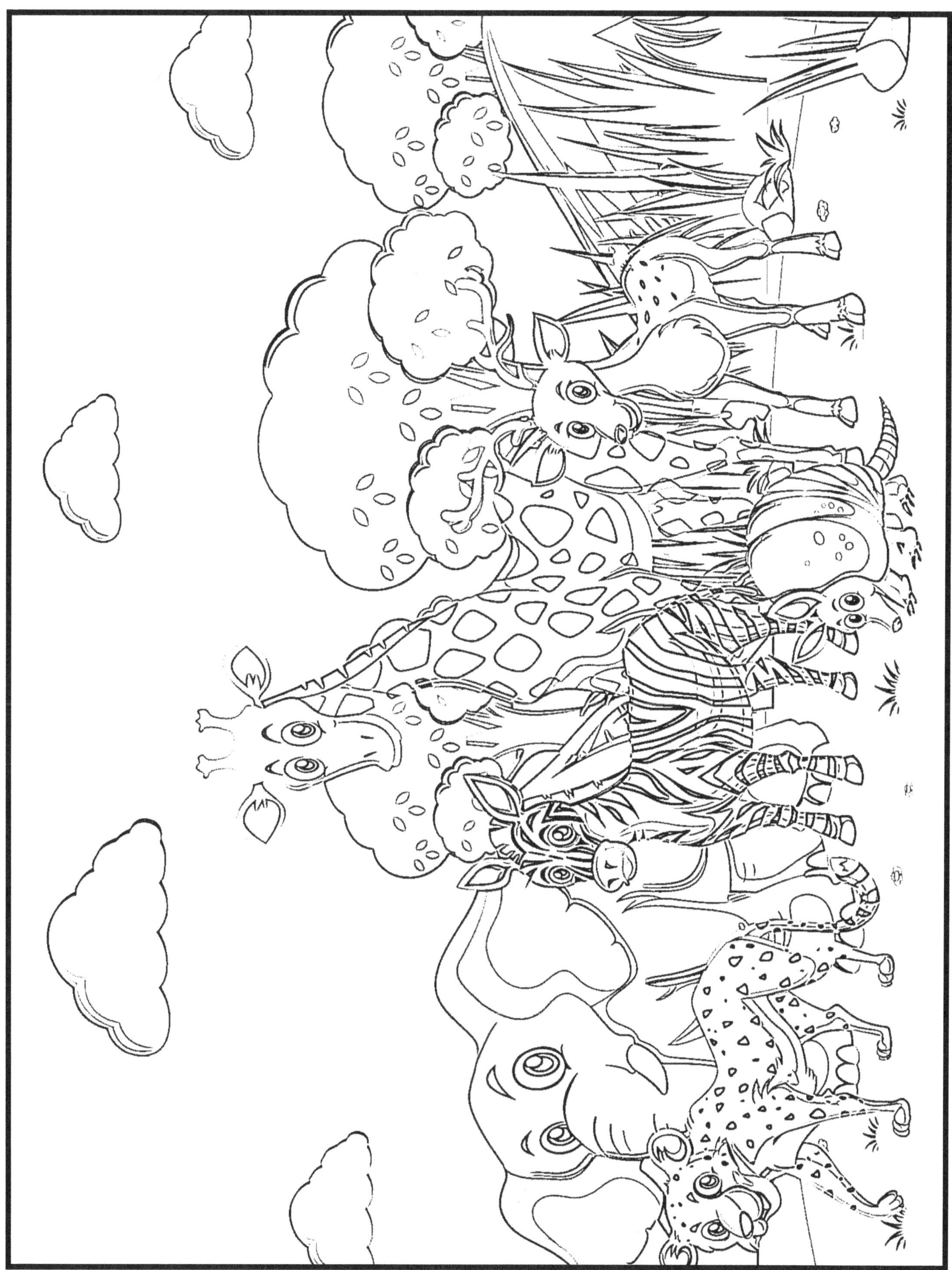

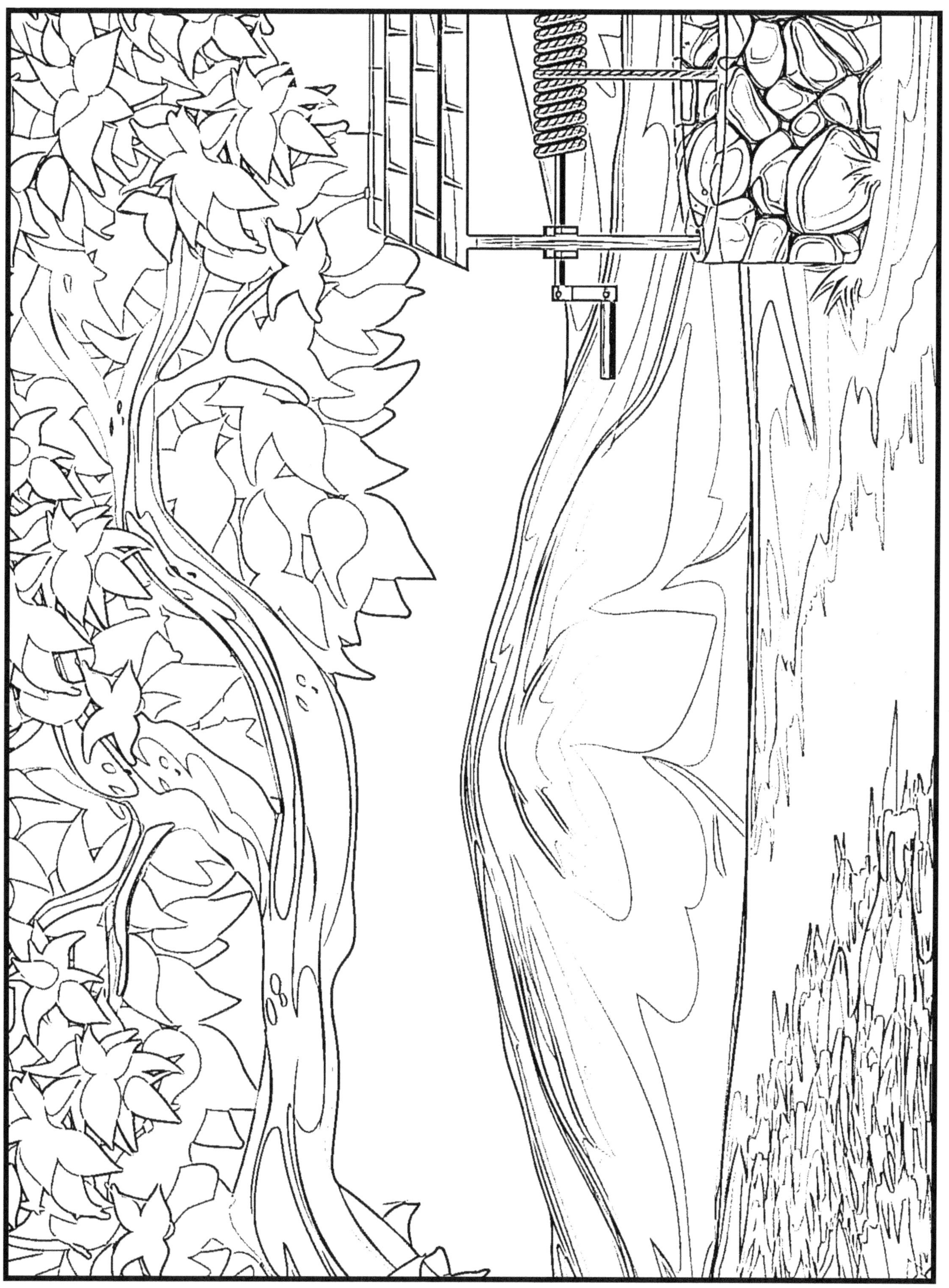

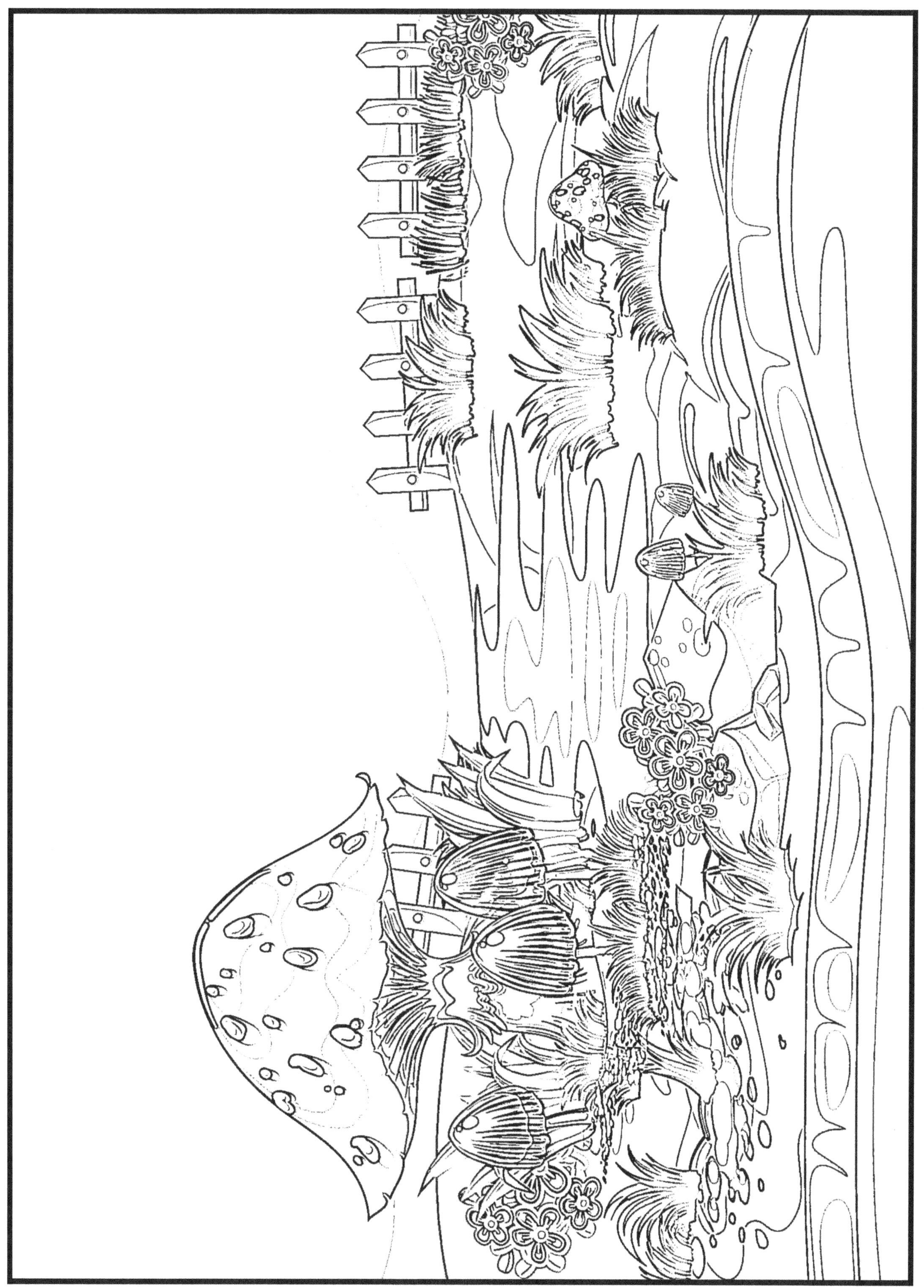

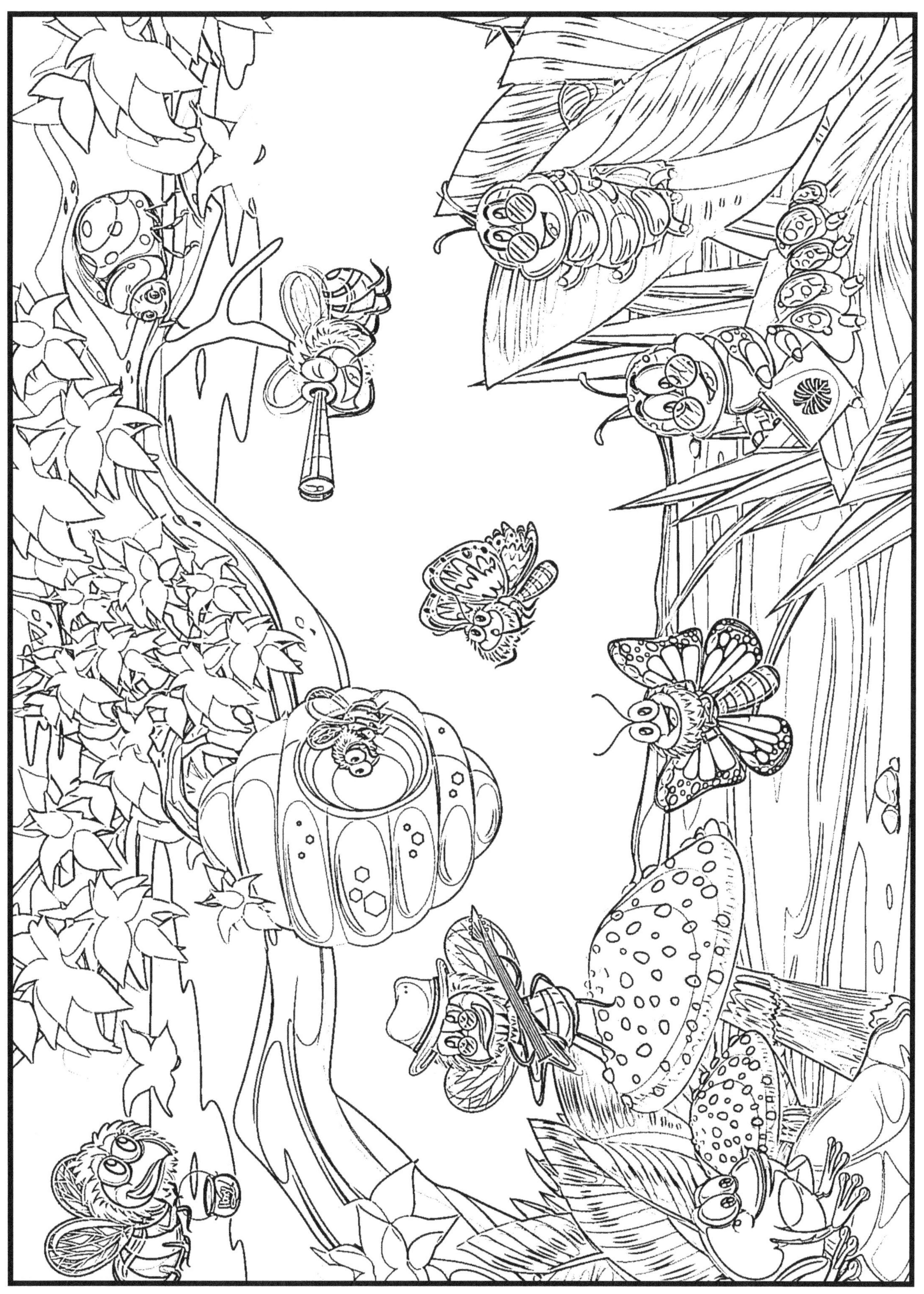

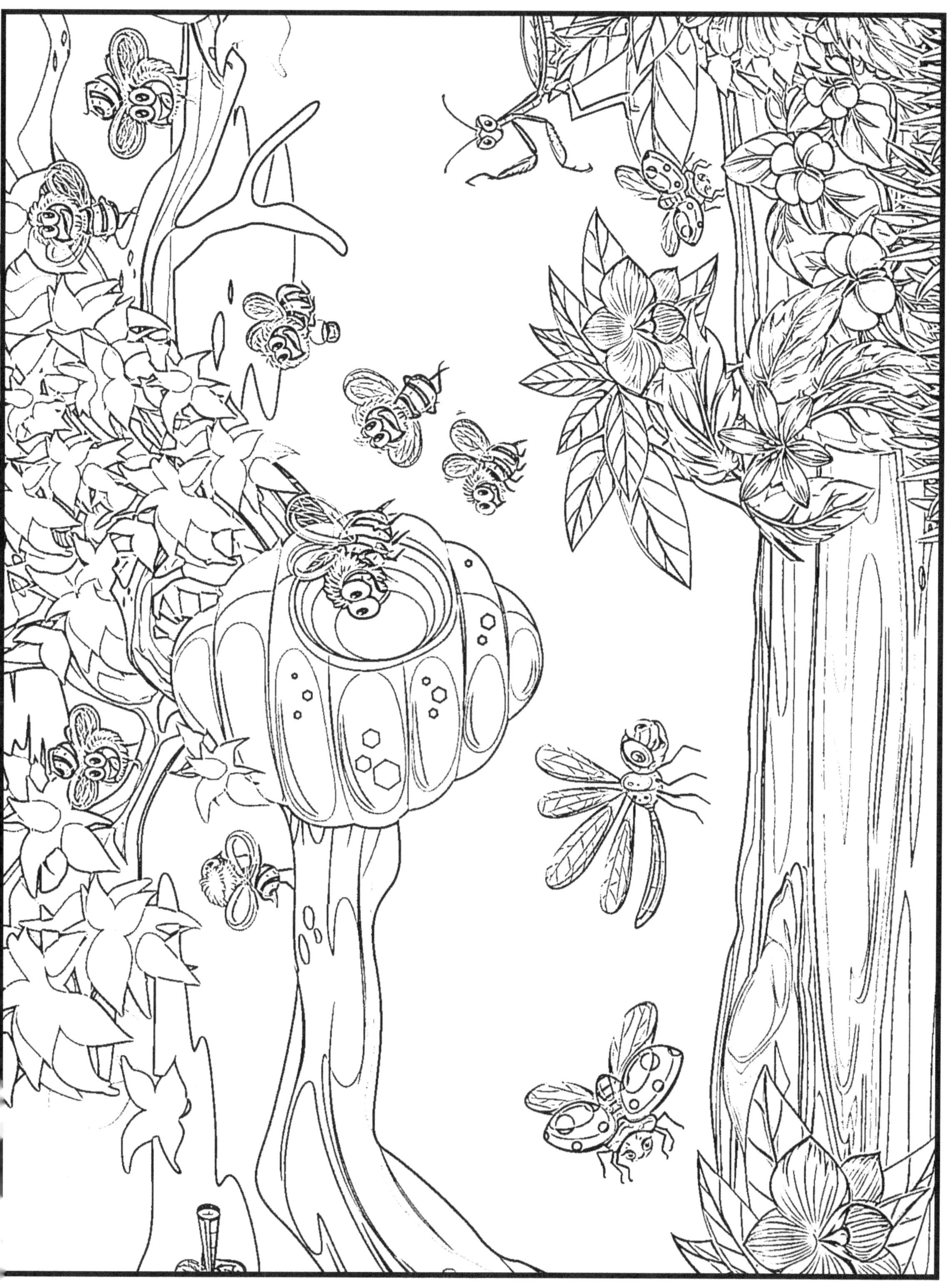

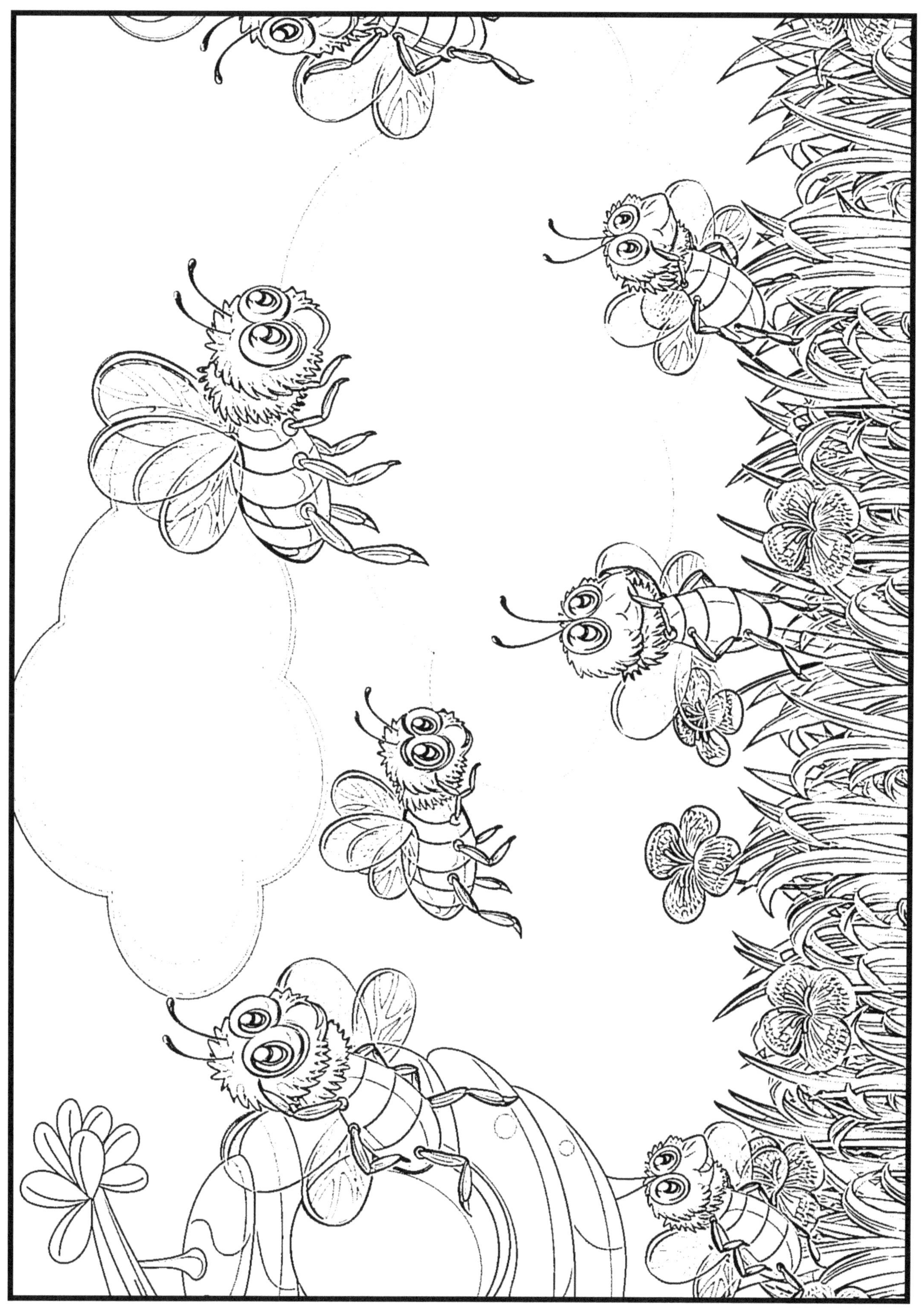

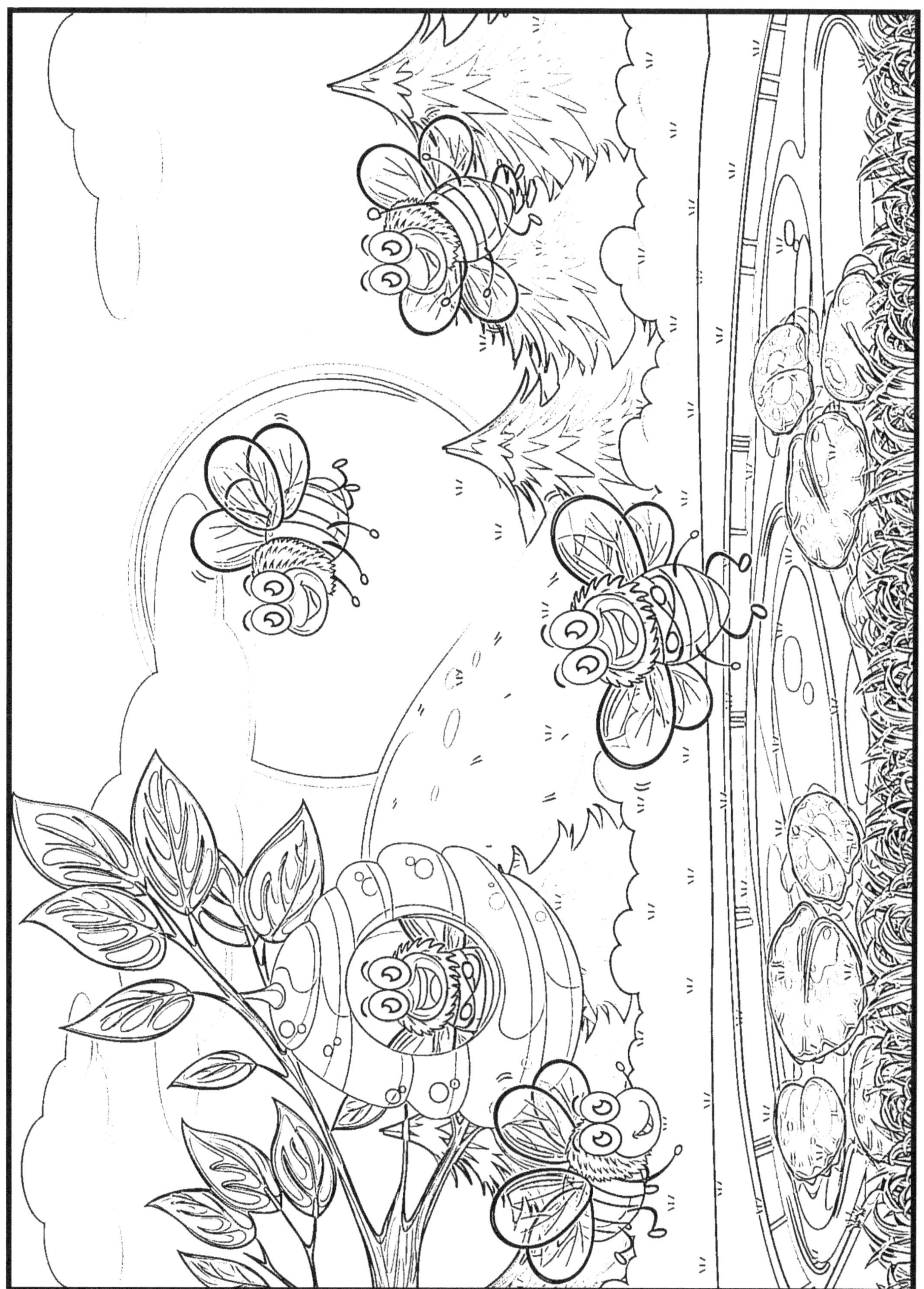

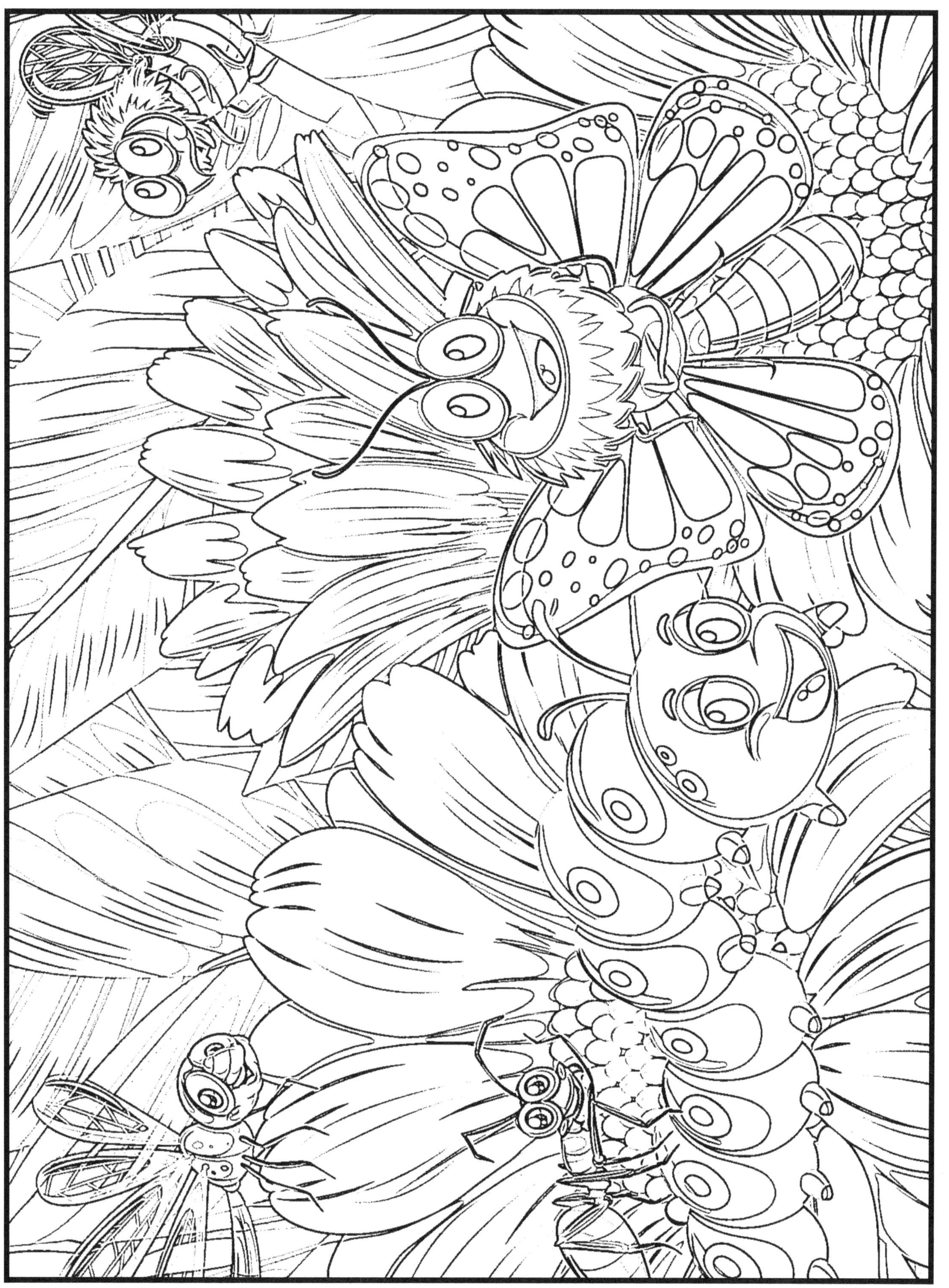

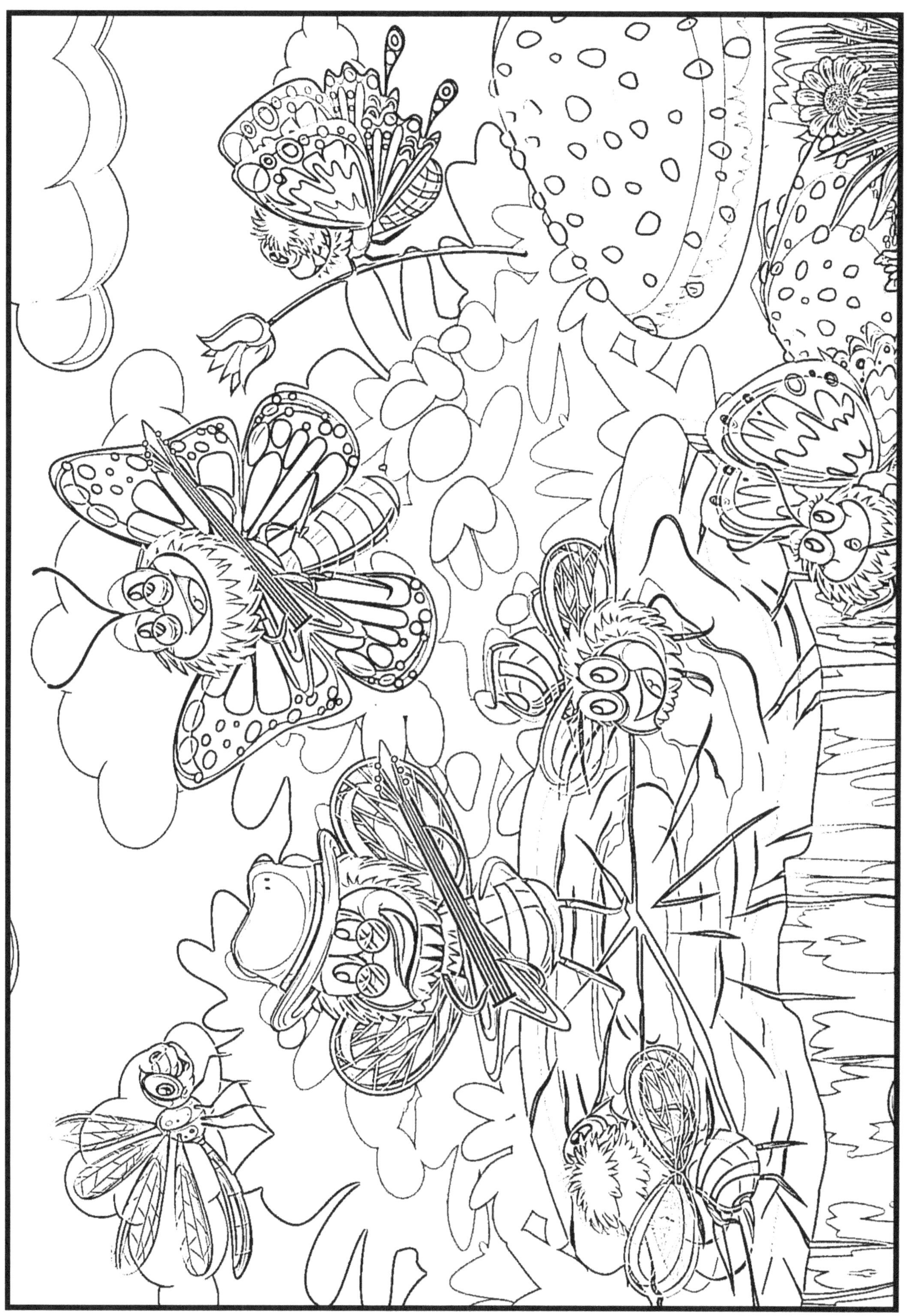

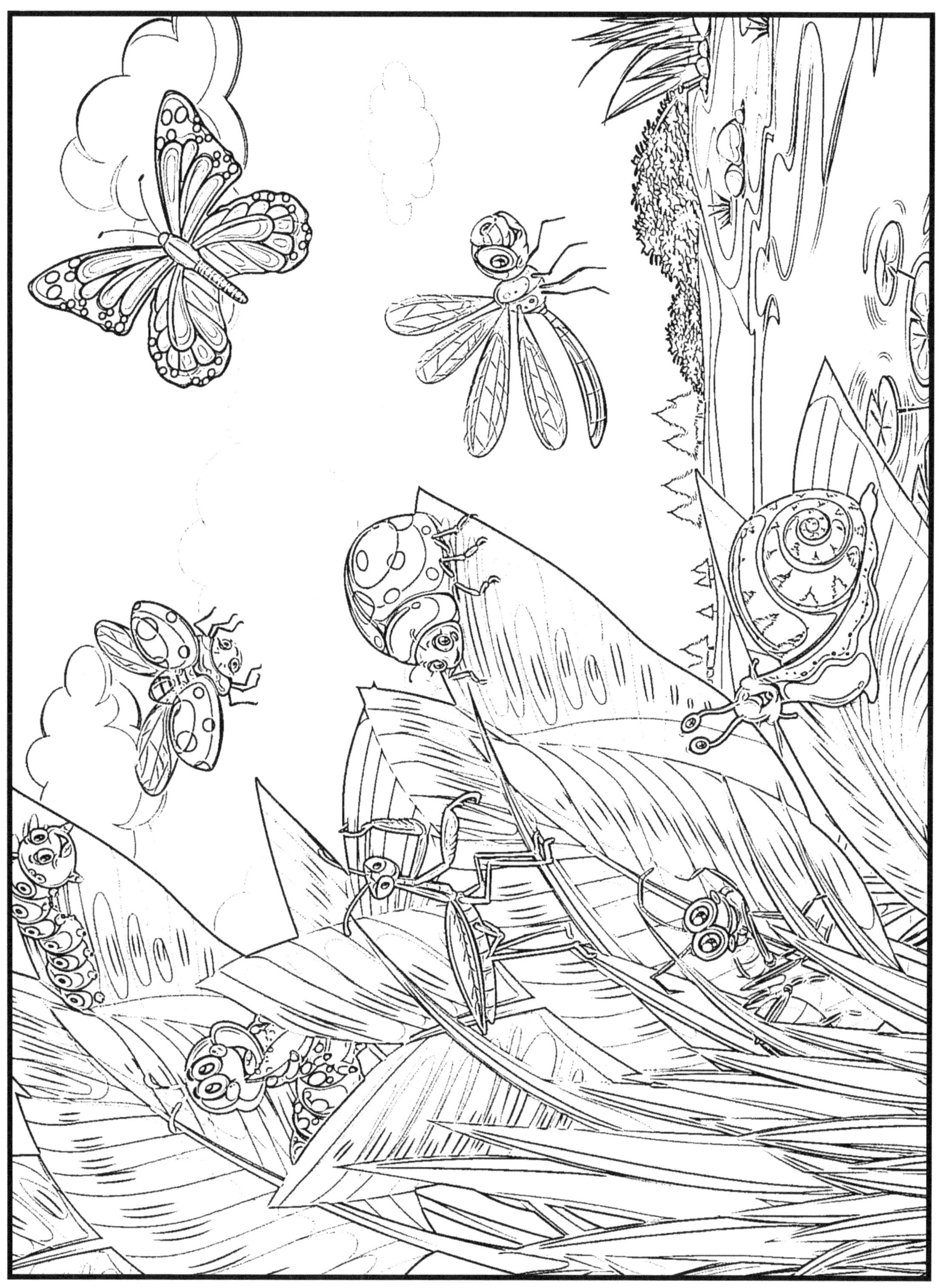

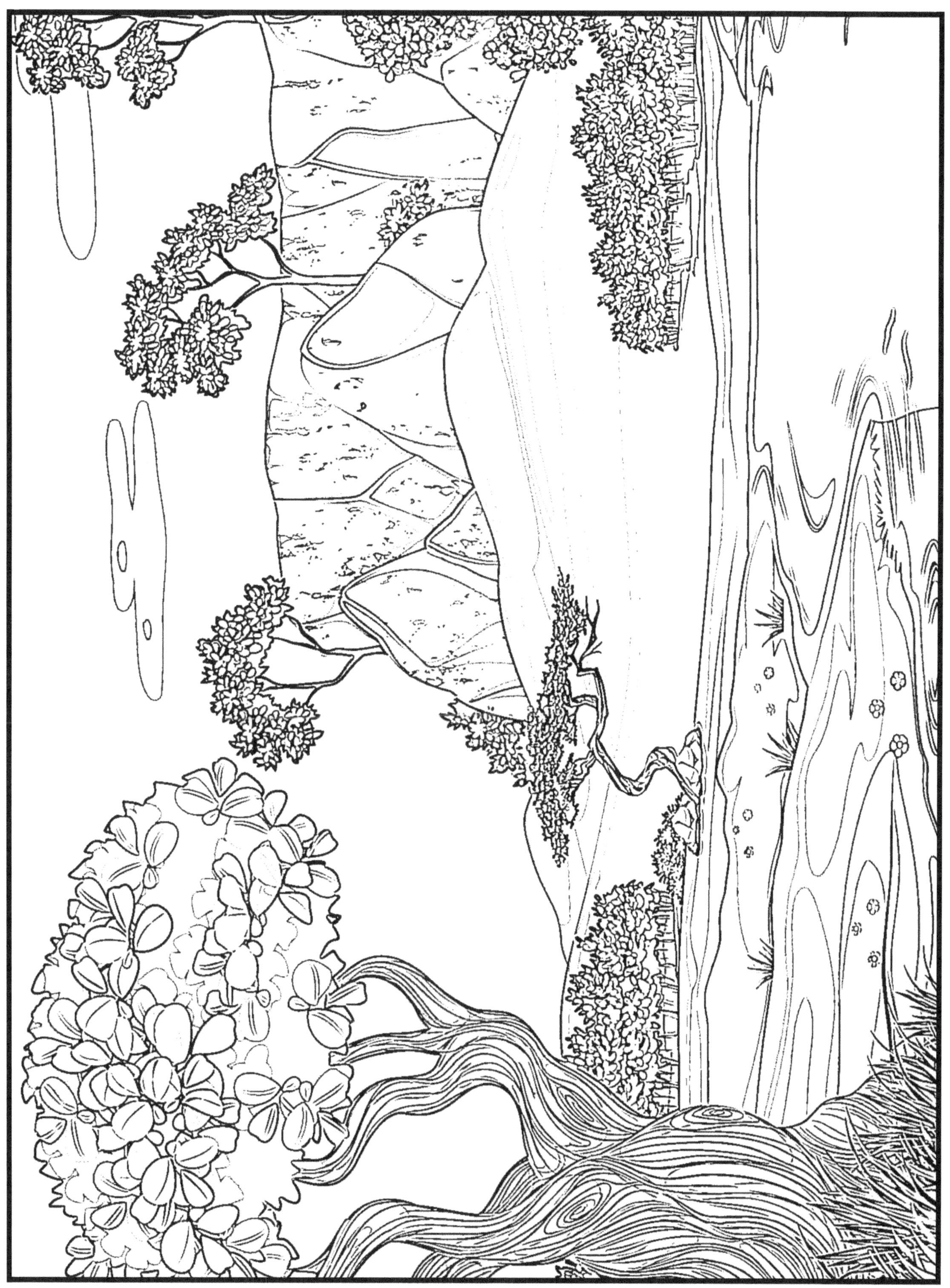

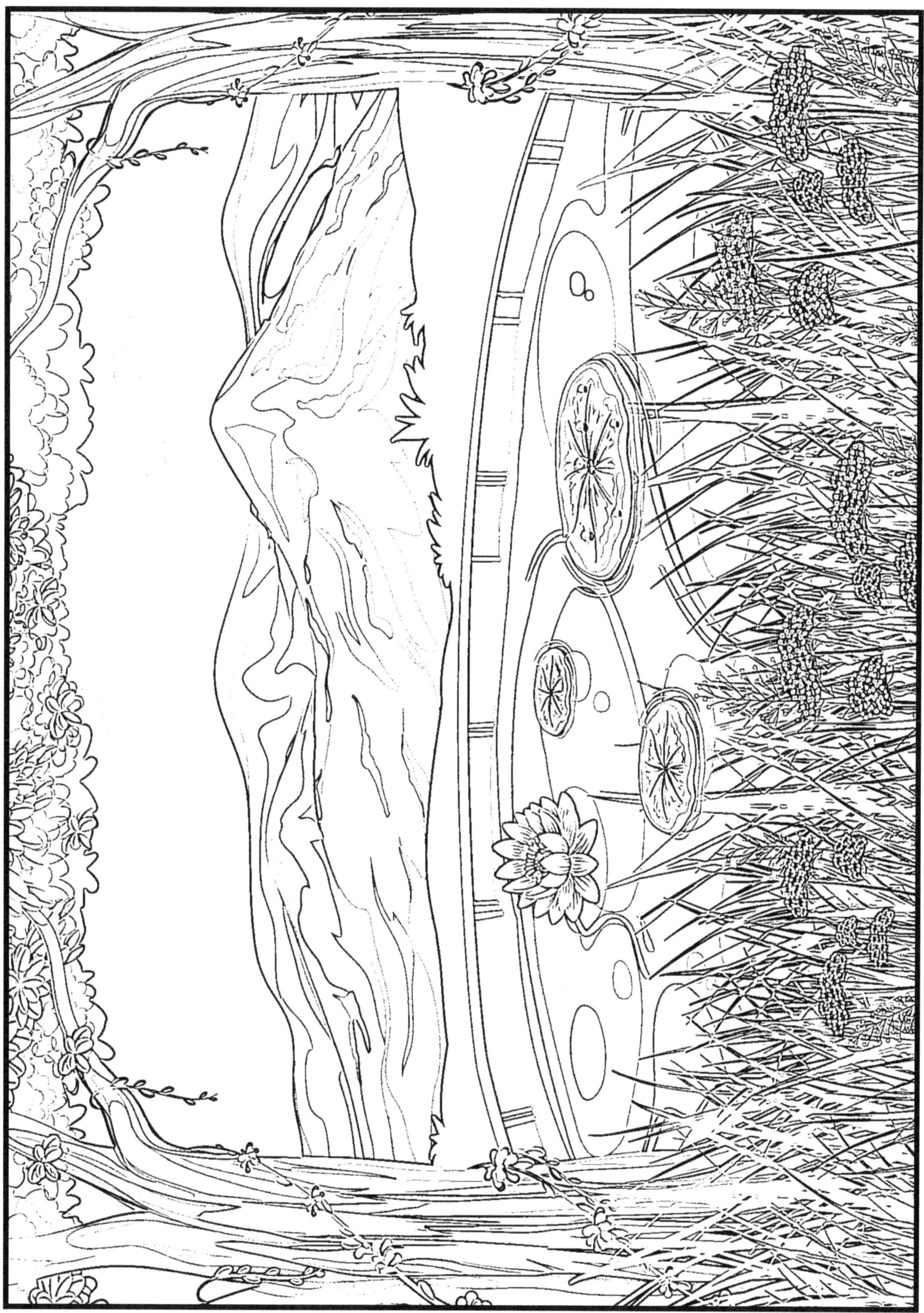

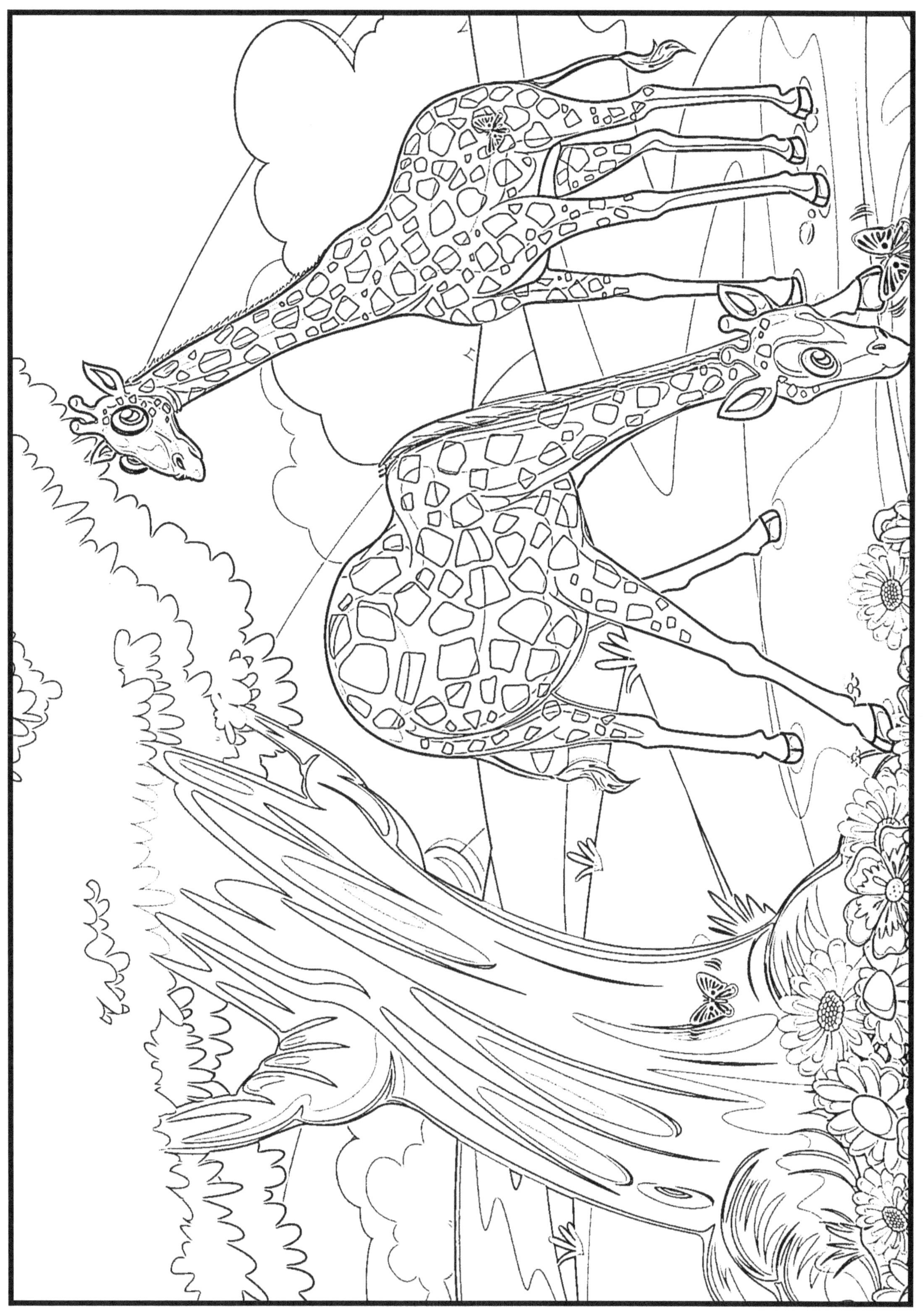

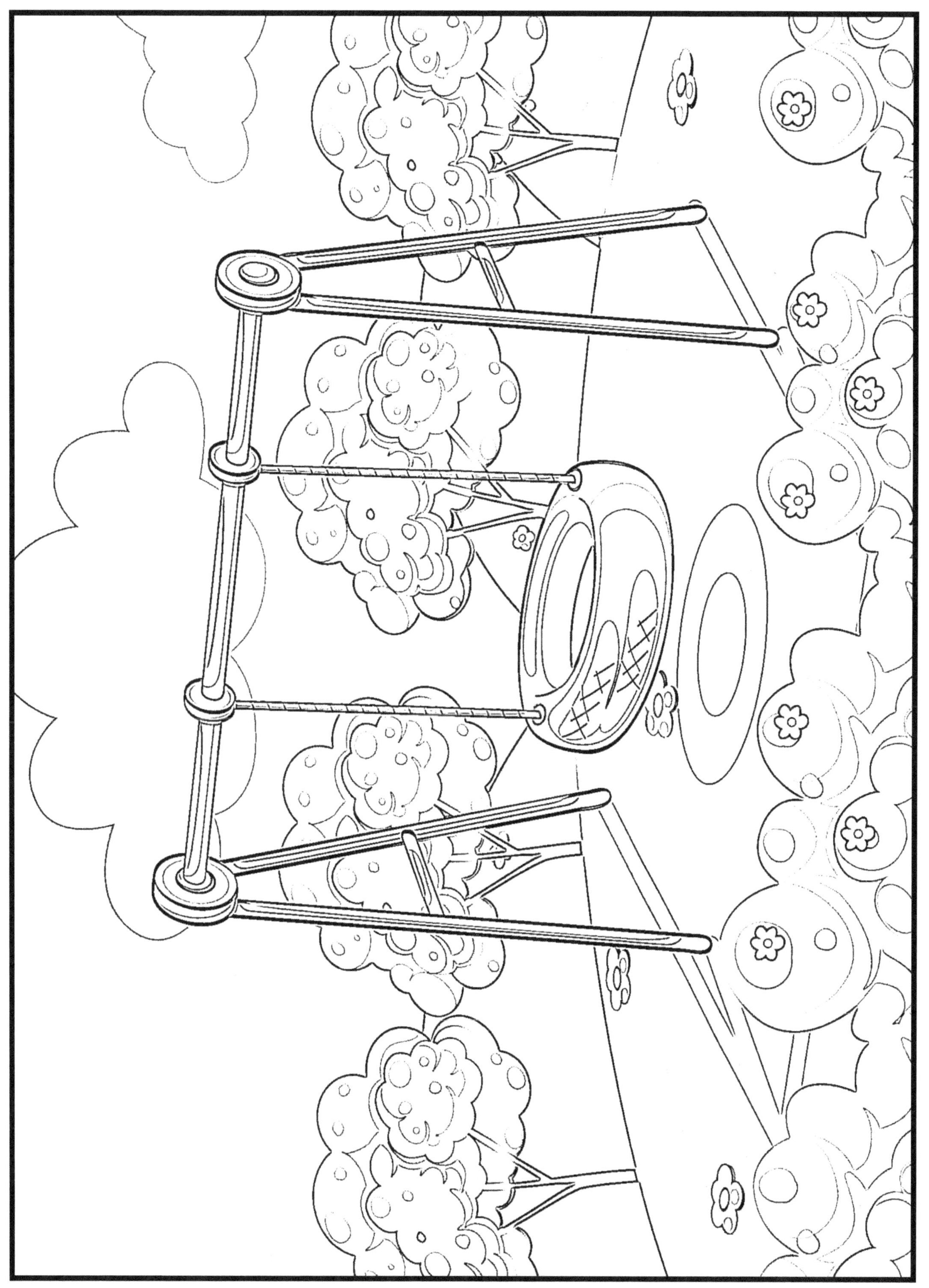

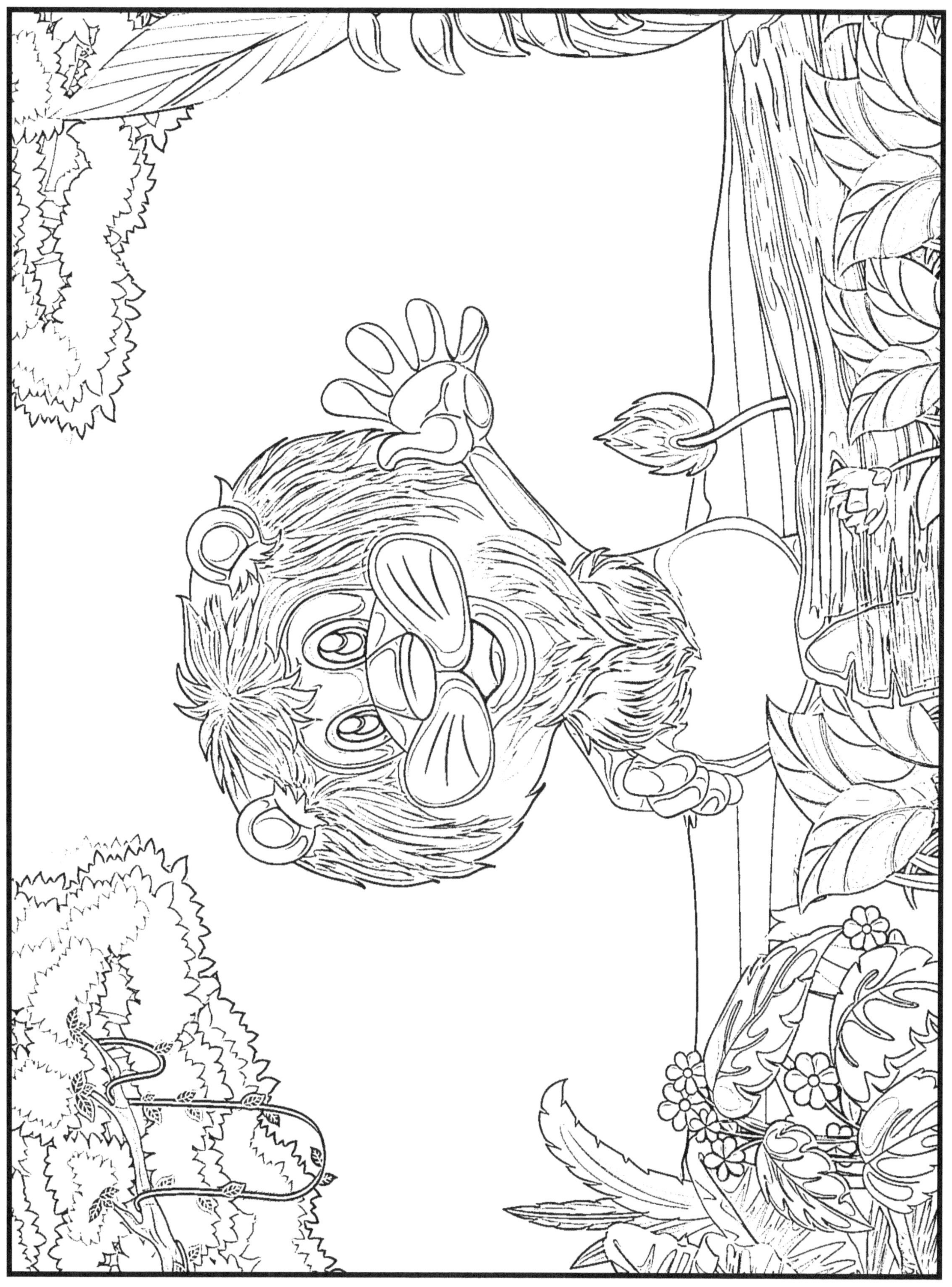

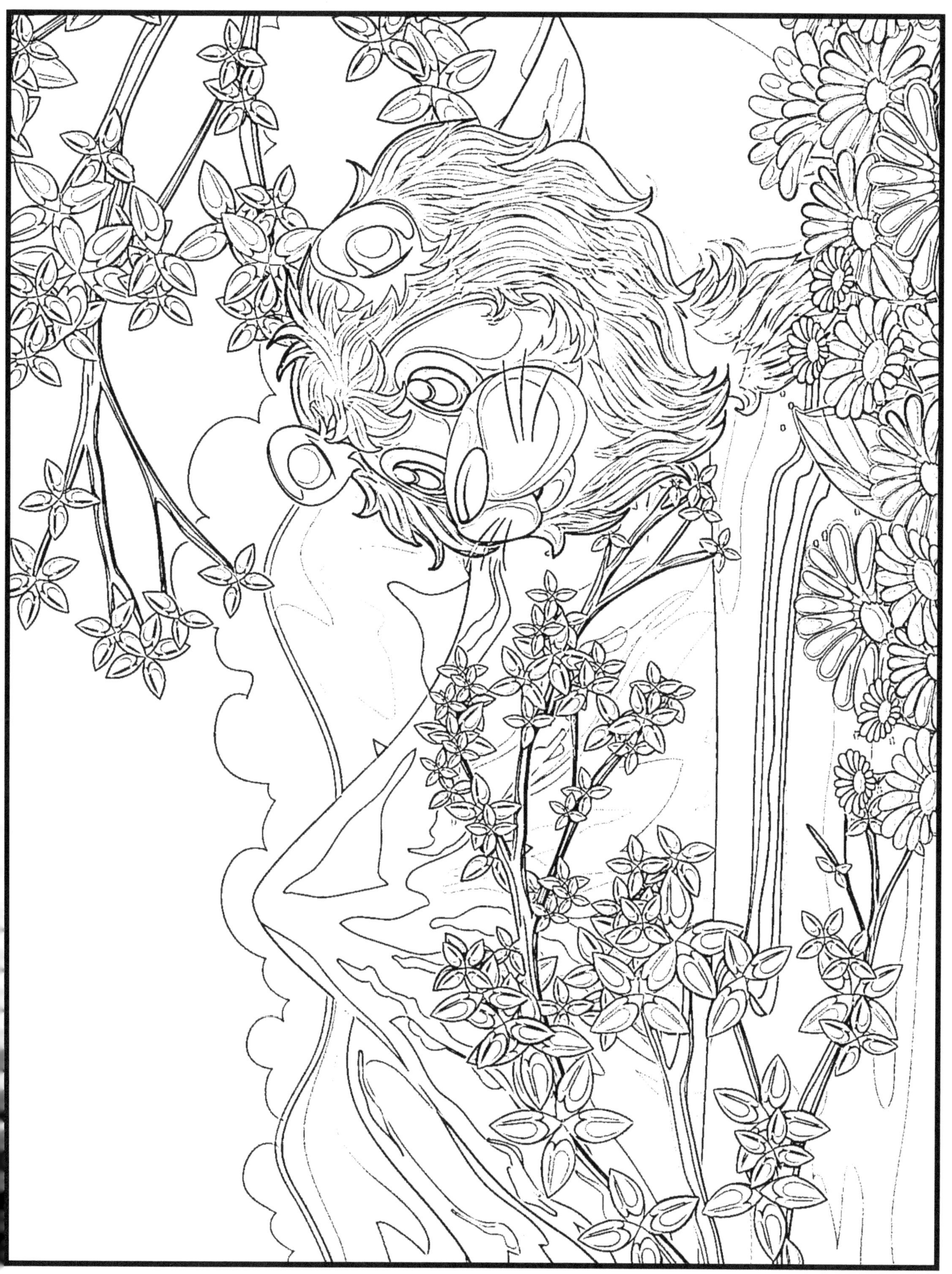

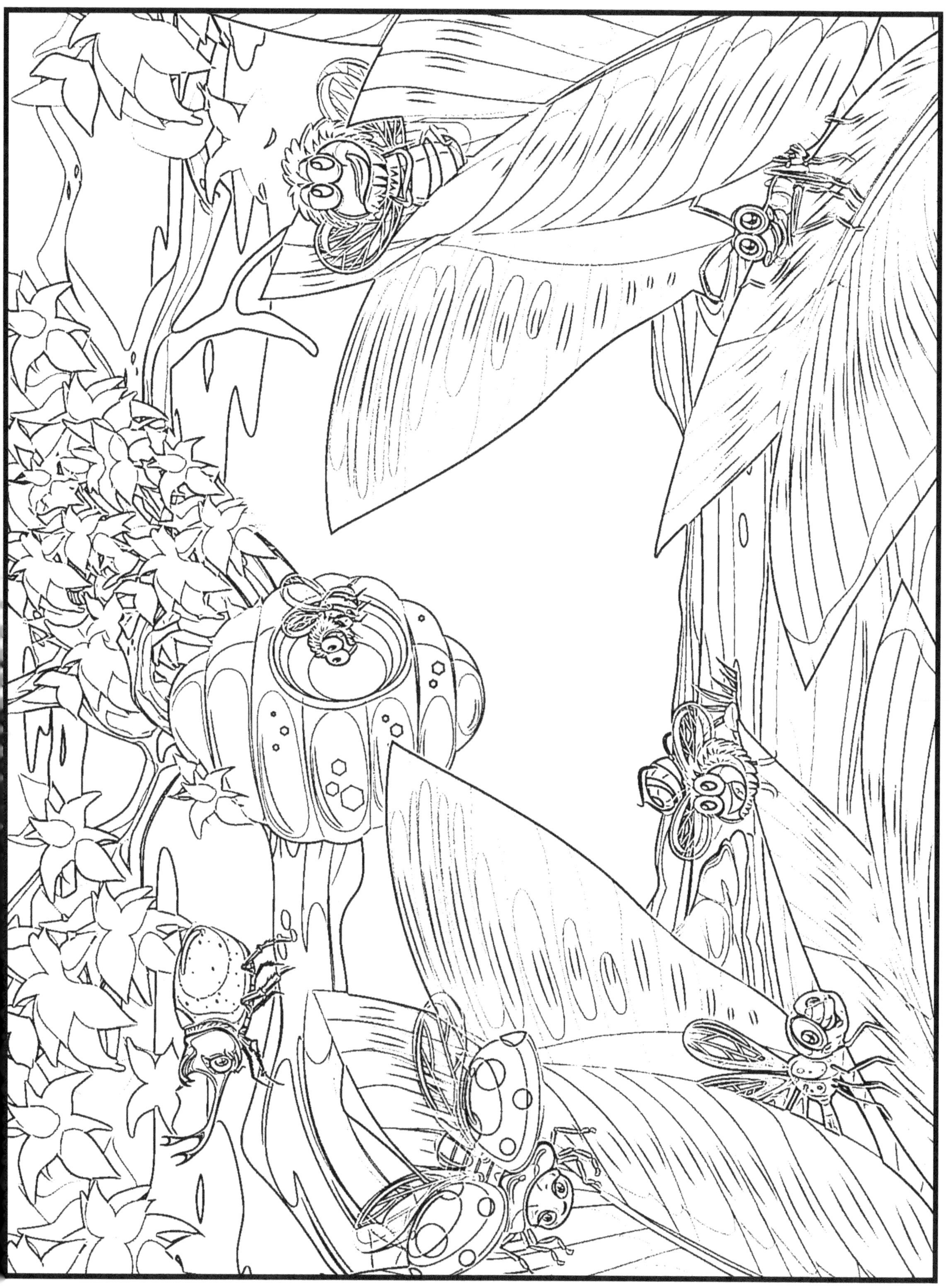

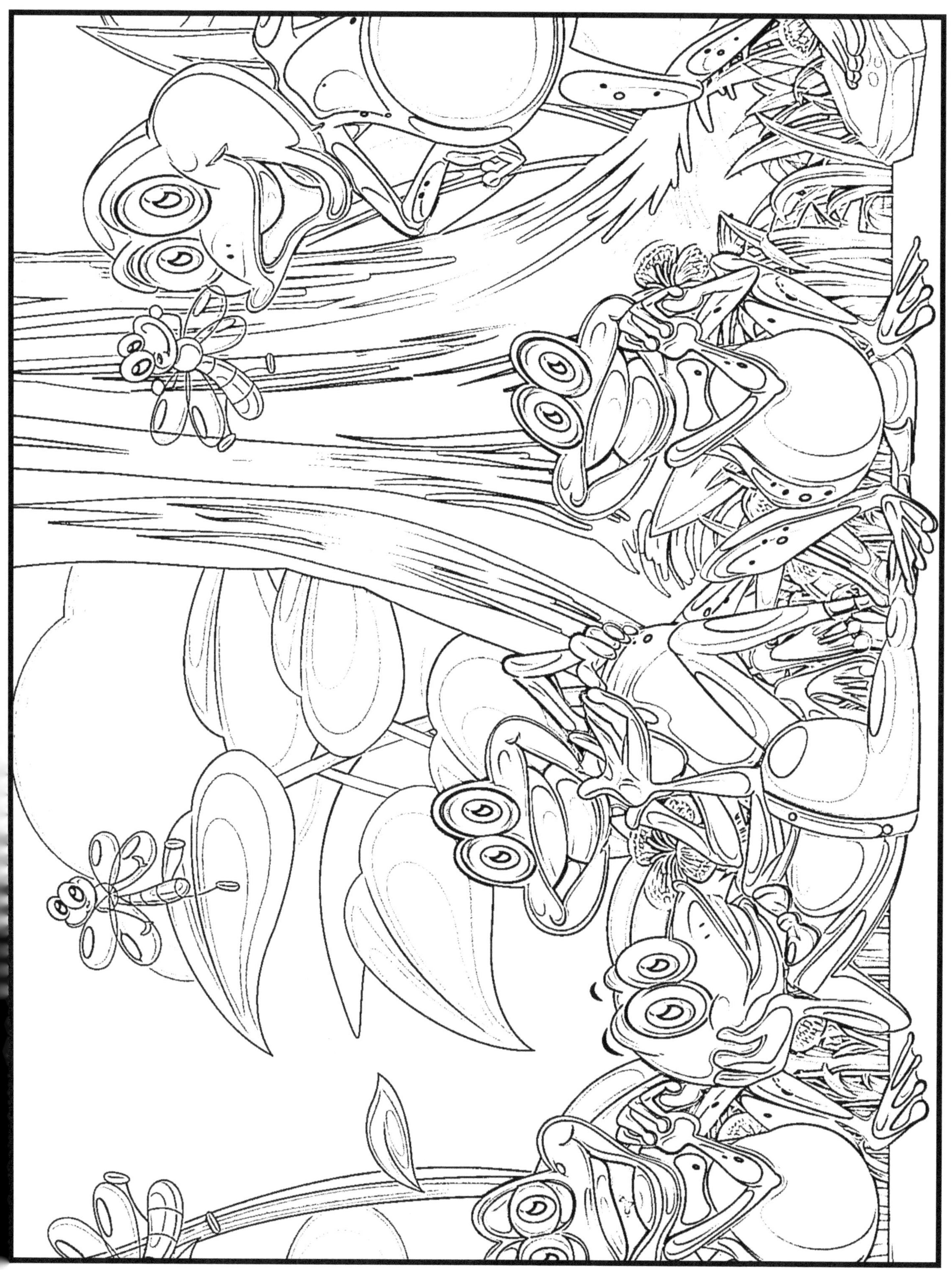

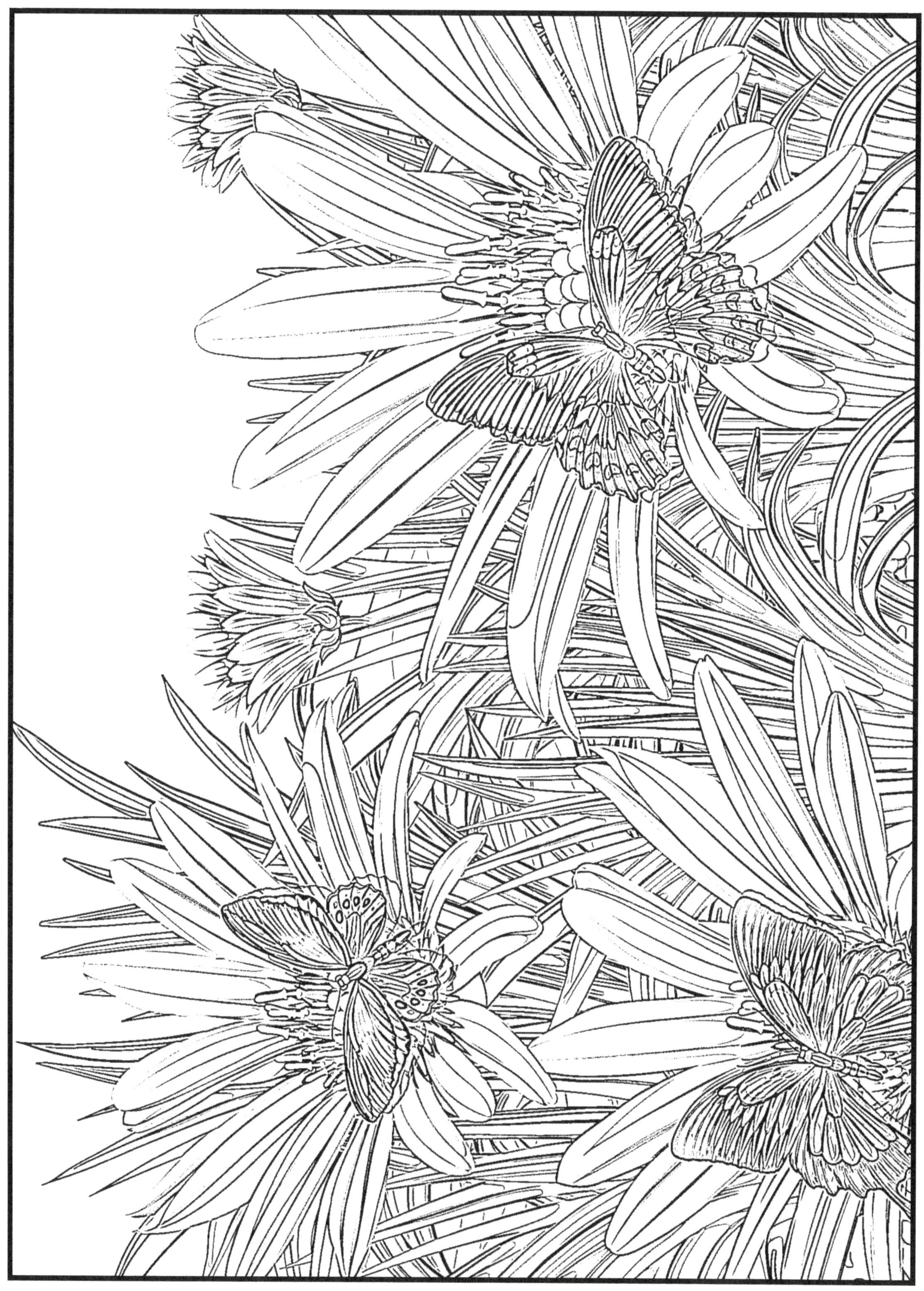

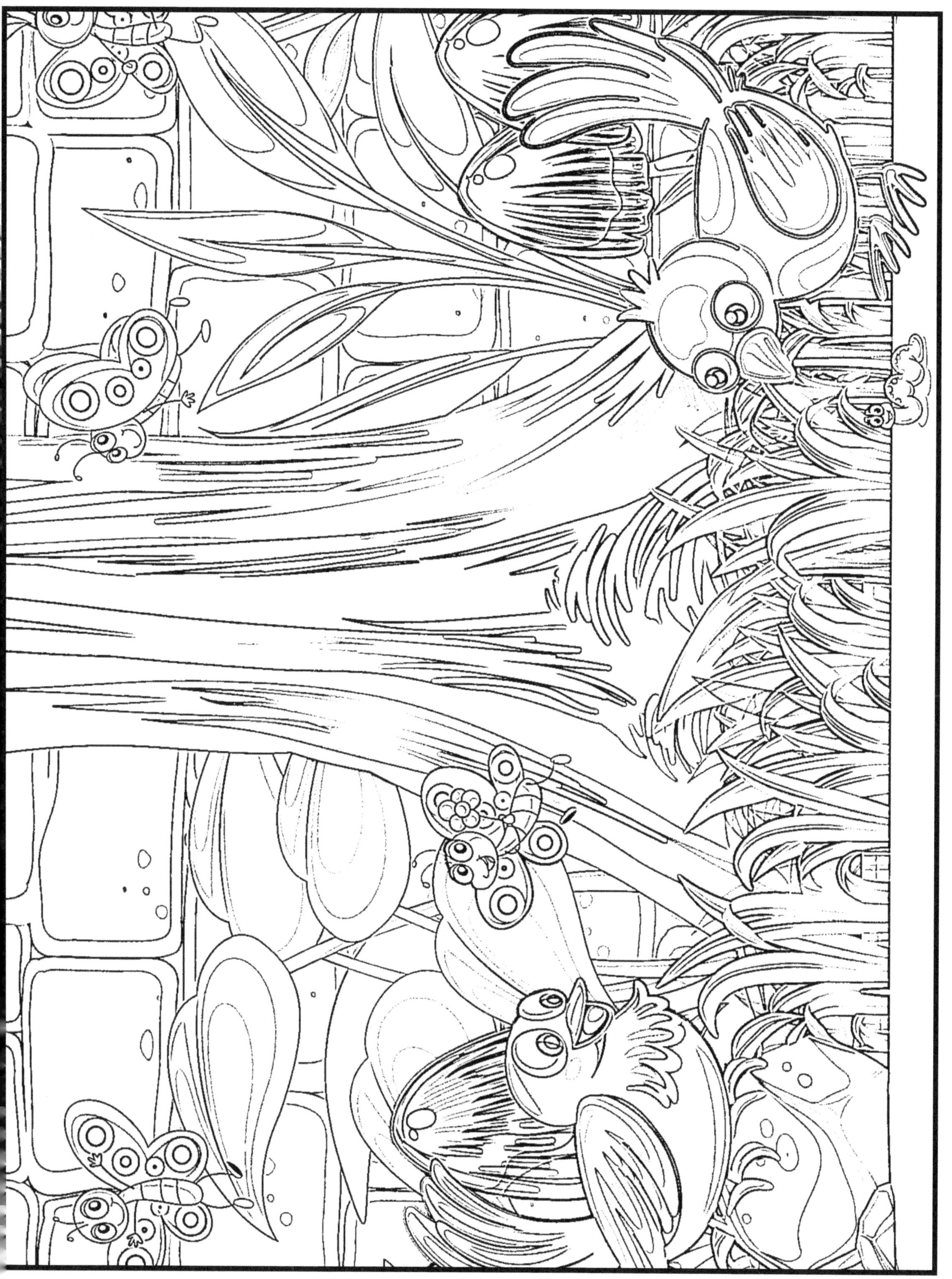

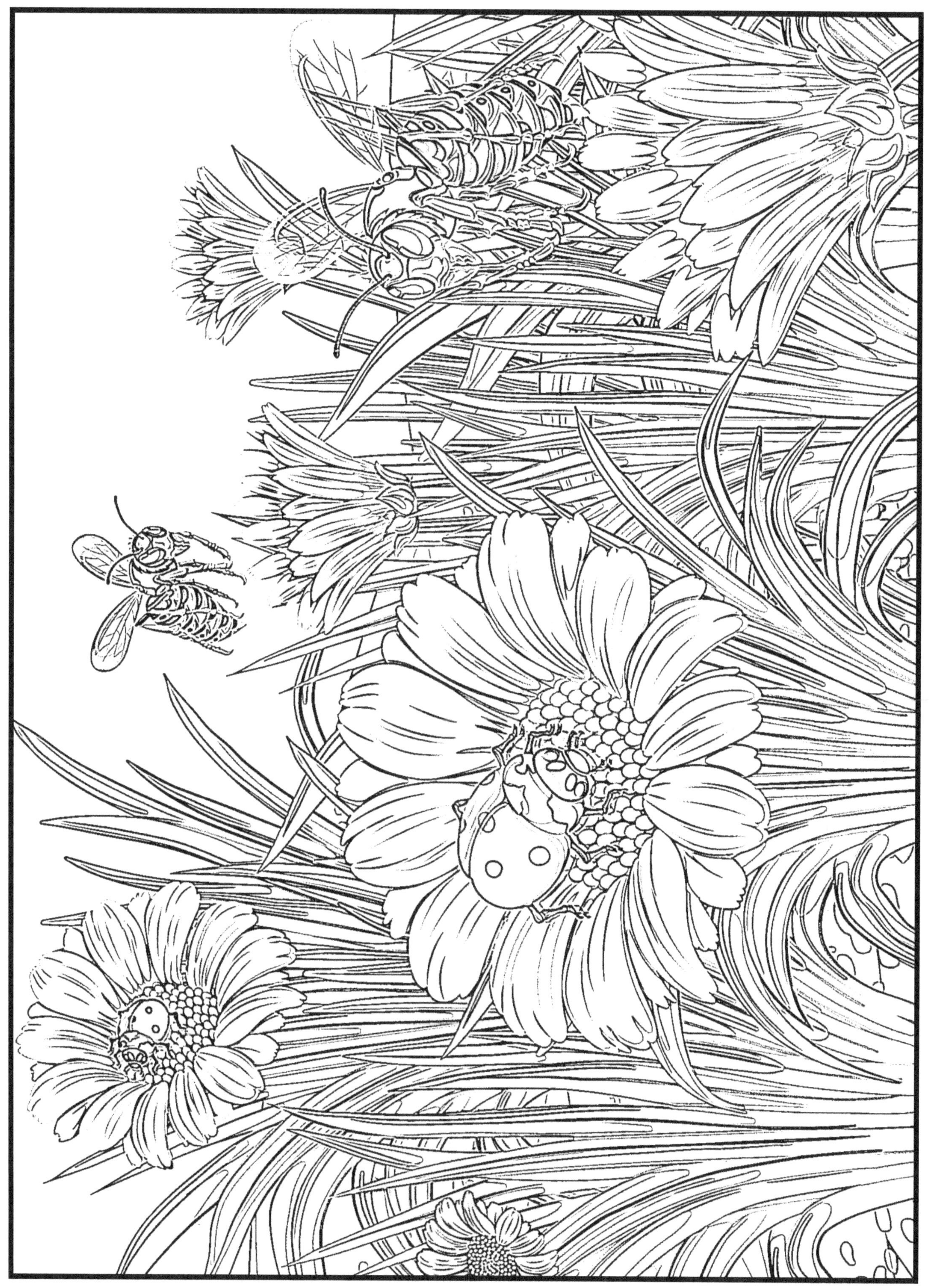

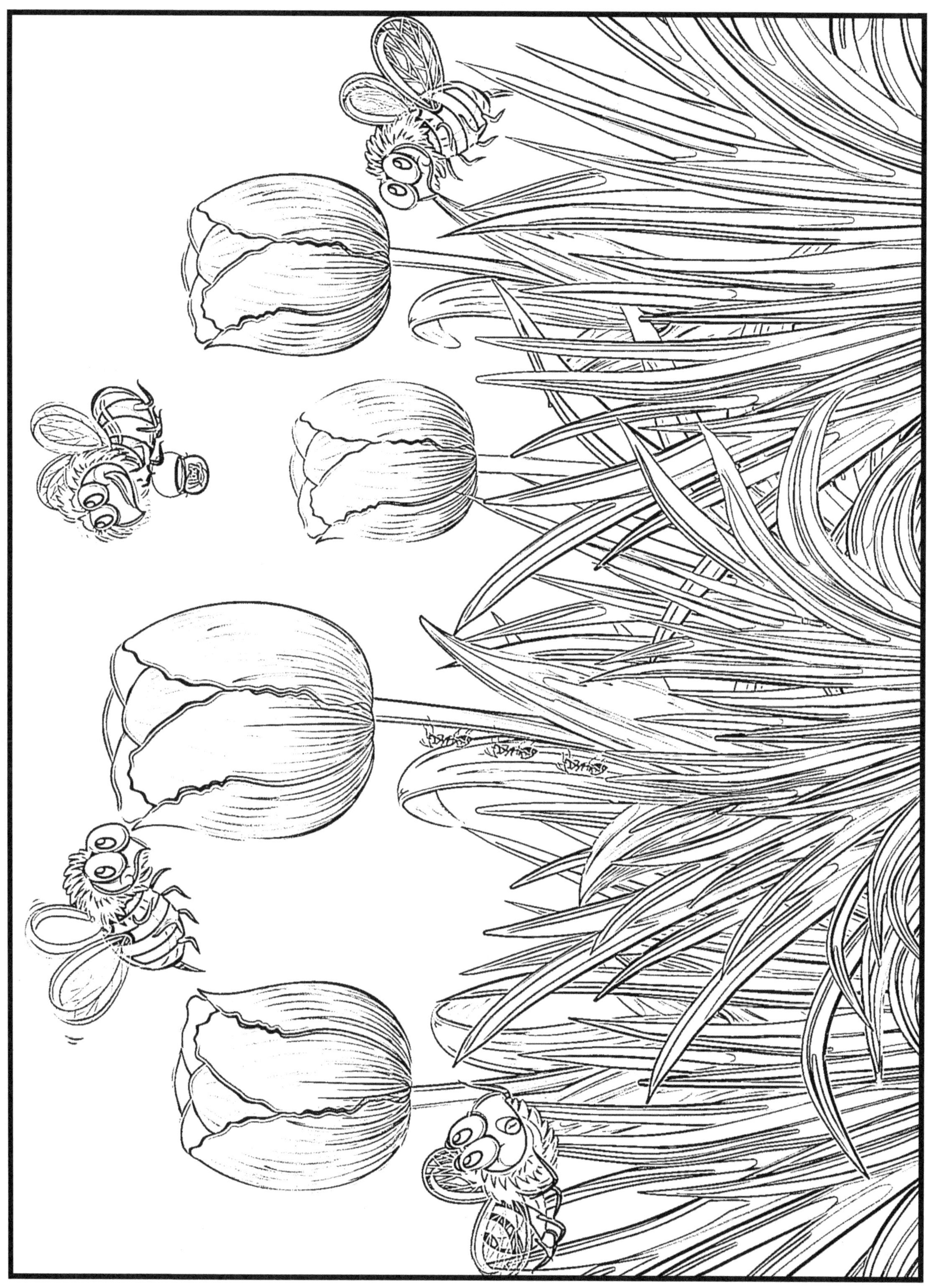

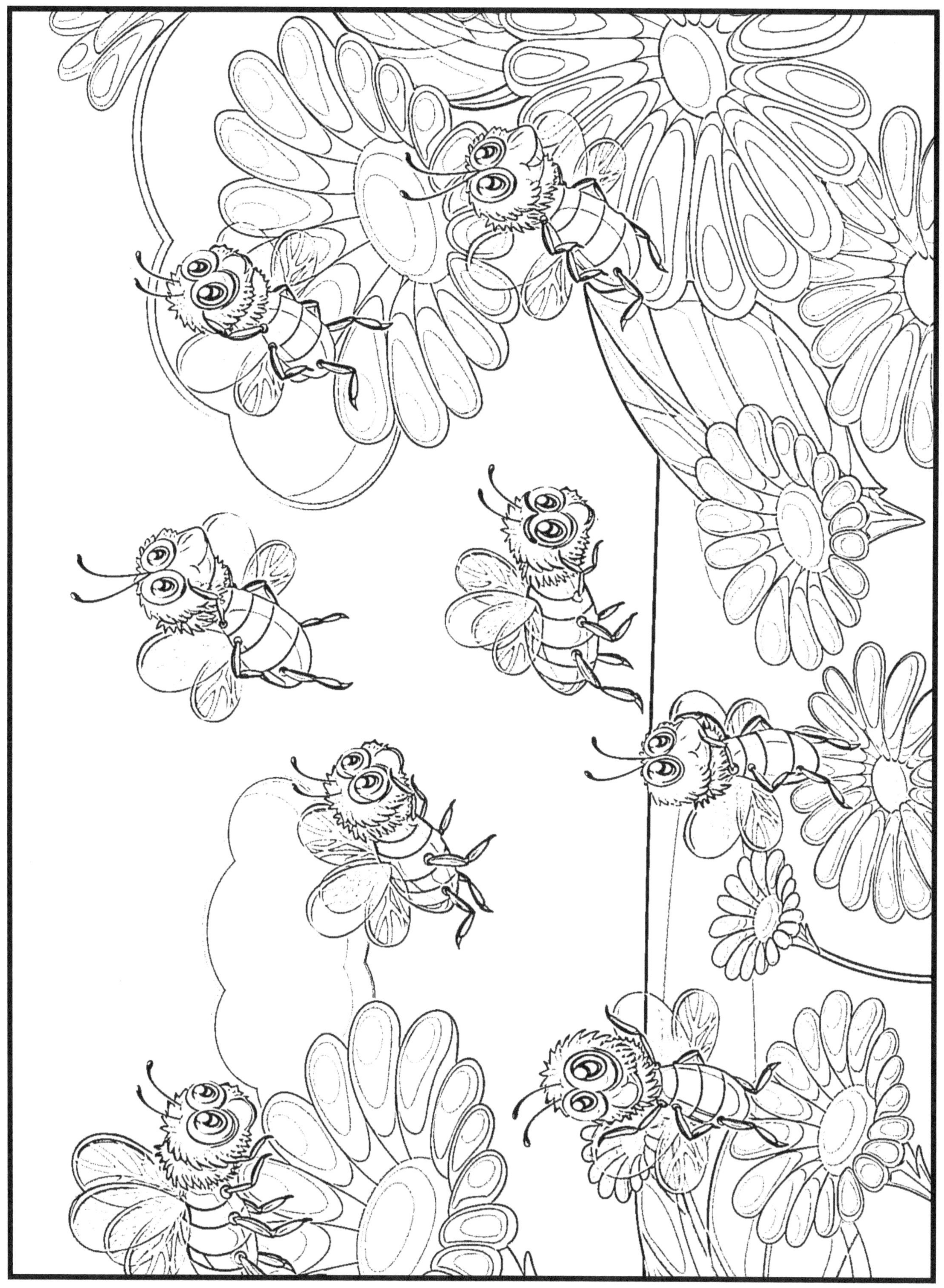

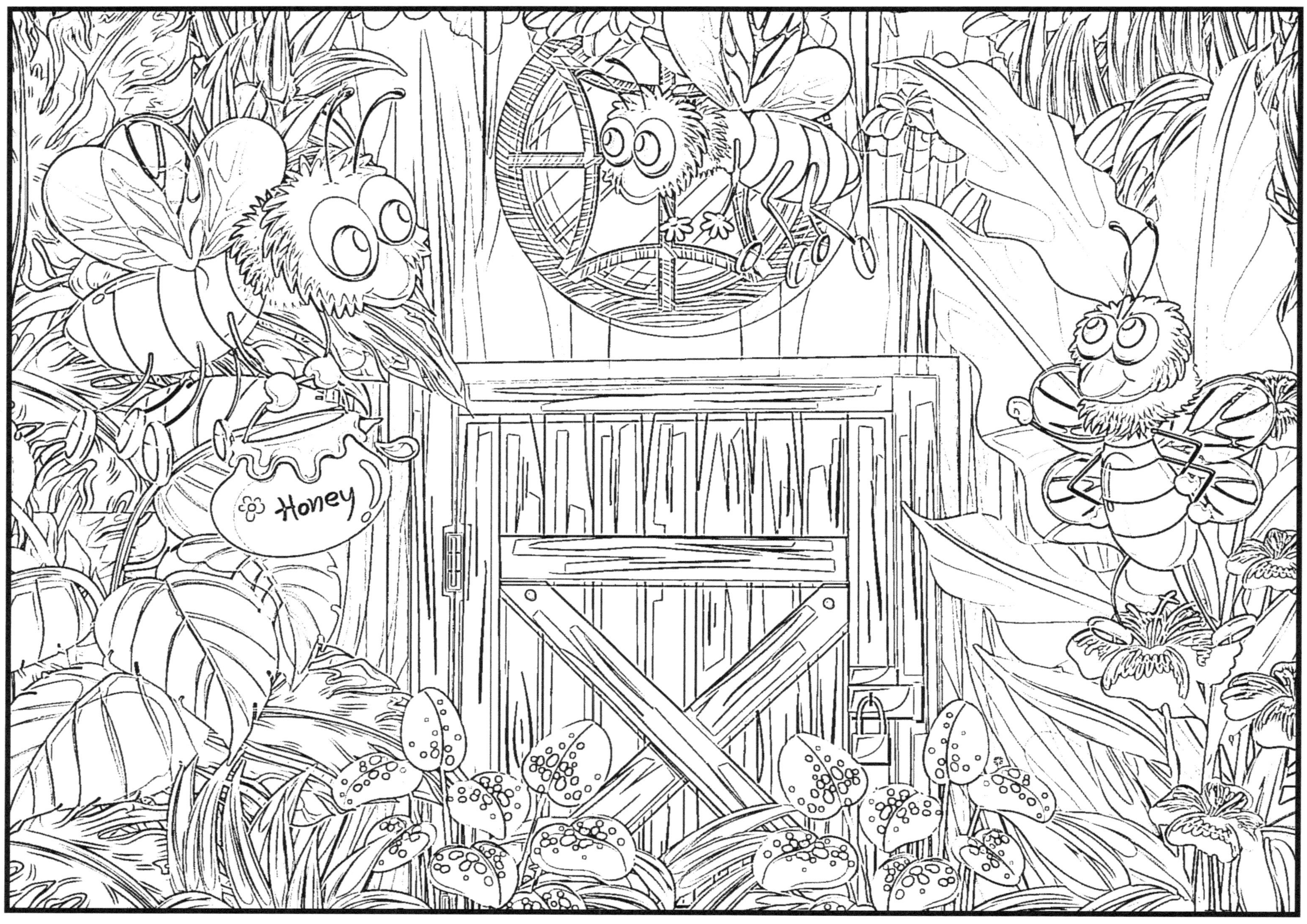

Honey